The Library
IN EAST AYRSHIRE

East Ayrshire
COUNCIL
Neighbourhood Services

Please return item by last date shown,
or contact library to renew

Festivals

My Easter

Monica Hughes

Heinemann
LIBRARY

Little Nippers

www.heinemann.co.uk/library
Visit our website to find out more information about **Heinemann Library** books.

To order:
☎ Phone 44 (0) 1865 888066
🖹 Send a fax to 44 (0) 1865 314091
💻 Visit the Heinemann Bookshop at www.heinemann.co.uk/library to browse our
catalogue and order online.

First published in Great Britain by Heinemann
Library, Halley Court, Jordan Hill, Oxford
OX2 8EJ, part of Harcourt Education.
Heinemann is a registered trademark of Harcourt
Education Ltd.

© Harcourt Education Ltd 2005
The moral right of the proprietor has been
asserted.

Editorial: Sarah Eason and Louise Galpine
Design: Jo Hinton-Malivoire and Tokay,
  Bicester, UK (www.tokay.co.uk)
Picture Research: Ruth Blair
Production: Severine Ribierre

Originated by Dot Gradations Ltd
Printed and bound in China by South China
Printing Company

ISBN 0 431 16261 1 (hardback)
09 08 07 06 05
10 9 8 7 6 5 4 3 2 1

ISBN 0 431 16265 4 (paperback)
09 08 07 06 05
10 9 8 7 6 5 4 3 2 1

British Library Cataloguing in Publication Data
Hughes, Monica
Little Nippers Festivals My Easter
263.9'3
A full catalogue record for this book is available
from the British Library.

Acknowledgements
The Publishers would like to thank the following
for permission to reproduce photographs: all
pictures Harcourt Education/Tudor Photography.

Cover photograph of Easter bonnets reproduced
with permission of Harcourt Education/Tudor
Photography.

The Publishers would like to thank Philip Emmett
for his assistance in the preparation of this book.

Every effort has been made to contact copyright
holders of any material reproduced in this book.
Any omissions will be rectified in subsequent
printings if notice is given to the Publishers.

Contents

We all decorate
our eggs carefully.

Say cheese!

Don't we look **great** in our Easter bonnets?

Good Friday

We all go to church to pray and think about Jesus.

NEW TESTAMENT CHURCH OF GOD

ALL ARE WELCOME

Headley Gayle

Hello!

After church Gran reads us the Easter story about Jesus.

A quiet meal

It is my turn to say grace today.

We always eat fish on Good Friday.

Amen!

At church

First I meet the other children for Sunday school.

Then we all go into church...

Let's celebrate!

We all worship together.

Pastor Gayle leads us all in singing 'Christ arise'.

A happy time

Now it's our time to lead the singing.

A wonderful meal

I'm helping to get the table ready for our Easter supper.

Everything **looks** and **smells** delicious.

Cards and presents

We give each other cards to **celebrate** Easter.

Now it's time to eat our Easter eggs.

21

Time for bed

Goodnight!

22

We've had a **wonderful** Easter.

Index

The end

Notes for adults

Most festivals and celebrations share common elements that will be familiar to the young child, such as new clothes, special food, sending and receiving cards and presents, giving to charity, being with family and friends and a busy and exciting build-up time. It is important that the child has an opportunity to compare and contrast their own experiences with those of the children in the book.

The following Early Learning Goals are relevant to this series:

Knowledge and understanding of the world
• Early learning goals for exploration and investigation: Discuss events that occur regularly within the children's experience, for example seasonal patterns, daily routines, celebrations

Personal, social and emotional development
• Early learning goals for a sense of community
• Respond to significant experiences, showing a range of feelings when appropriate
• Have a developing respect for their own cultures and beliefs and those of other people

Easter is a weeklong Christian festival that celebrates the death and the resurrection of Jesus Christ. Lent begins forty days earlier on Ash Wednesday. Easter takes place in March or April and is celebrated with symbols of new life including eggs and spring flowers. Special services are held in churches where prayers are said and joyous hymns are sung. The festival is also seen as a retail opportunity and shops sell a wide variety of goods linked to the celebration. Fairs, parades and marches are also common and new clothes are often worn. The celebration of Easter varies among Christian denominations. We have shown the celebrations of a Pentecostal church in this book.